THE ALL NEW STYLE OF MAGAZINE-BOOKS

SDM

www.SDMLIVE.com

MP

MOCY PUBLISHING
WWW.MOCYPUBLISHING.COM

REAL MUSIC. REAL ENTERTAINMENT.

S.DM

ISSUE 3

KOSTA
JUST HIT THE JACKPOT WITH A NEW SMASH HIT SINGLE "LOTTERY"

BIGG DAWG BLAST
LAUNCHES THE STREET HITTA DJ'S MOVEMENT

Neisha Neshae

BRINGING IN 2016 ON STAGE WITH THE KING OF R&B R-KELLY & DROPPING A NEW MIXTAPE

PLUS MORE

THE RED CARPET EDITION
SUPERSTARS CAME WITH FASHION AT THE SDM MAGAZINE RELEASE PARTY

US - $9.99 CANADA - $14.99

01 >

9 770317 847001

JANUARY 2016 No.3
WWW.SDMLIVE.COM

SDM

EDITOR-IN-CHIEF
D. "Casino" Bailey
casino@sdmlive.com

EDITORIAL DIRECTOR
Sheree Cranford
sheree@sdmlive.com

GRAPHIC/WEB DESIGNER
D. "Casino" Bailey
casino@sdmlive.com

A&R MANAGER
Aye Money
ayemoney@sdmlive.com

ACCOUNT EXECUTIVE
Frank Harvest Jr.
frank@sdmlive.com

PHOTOGRAPHERS
Treagen Colston
D. "Casino" Bailey

CONTRIBUTORS
April Smiley
Courtney Benjamin

COPY ORDERS & ADVERTISING OFFICE
Send Money Order or Check to:
Mocy Publishing
P.O. Box 35195
Detroit, Michigan 48235
(586) 646-8505
advertise@sdmlive.com

Copy Order Item #:
SDM Magazine Issue #8 2016
S&H Plus Retail Price - $9.99 per copy

WWW.SDMLIVE.COM

Printed by CreateSpace, An Amazon.com Company

MP
MOCY PUBLISHING

Copyright © 2016 Support Detroit Movement,
a division of Aye Money Promotions & Publishing, LLC and
Mocy Music Publishing, LLC. All rights reserved.
Printed in the U.S.A.

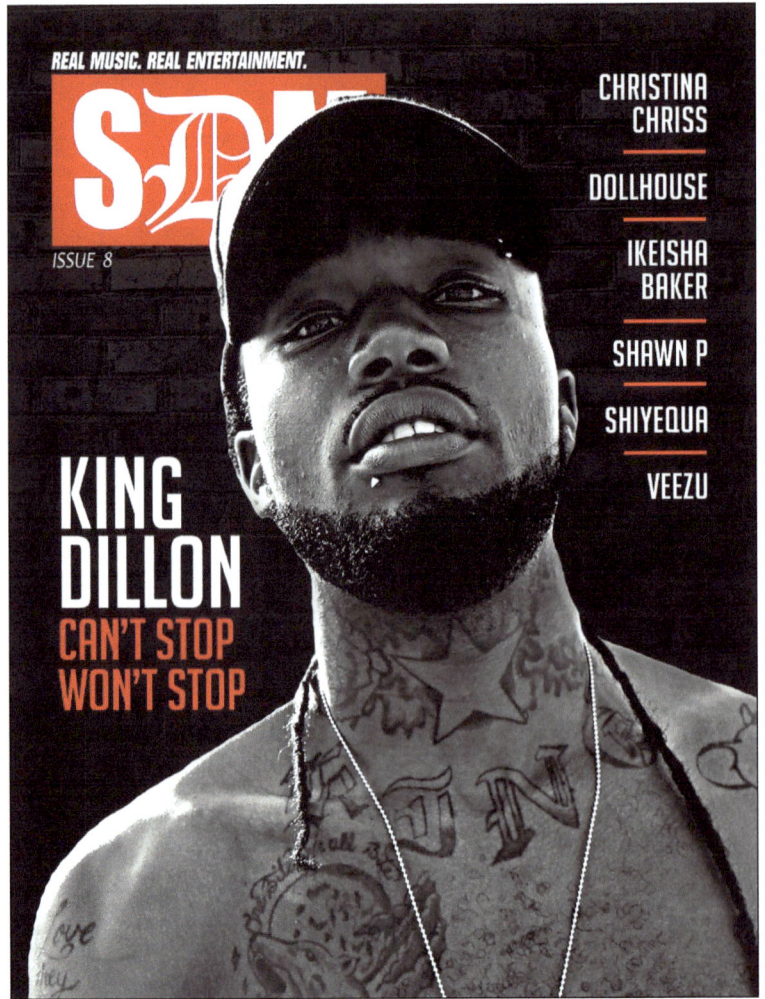

REAL MUSIC. REAL ENTERTAINMENT.

SDM

ISSUE 8

CHRISTINA CHRISS

DOLLHOUSE

IKEISHA BAKER

SHAWN P

SHIYEQUA

VEEZU

KING DILLON
CAN'T STOP WON'T STOP

CONTENTS

1

HP - ENVY 27" Touch-Screen All-In-One Intel Core i5 - 12GB Memory - 1TB Hard Drive - Silver $1,049.99
www.bestbuy.com

2

Samsung - SmartThings Hub - White
$79.99
www.bestbuy.com

3

Canon - MAXIFY MB2320 Wireless All-In-One Printer - Black
$99.99
www.bestbuy.com

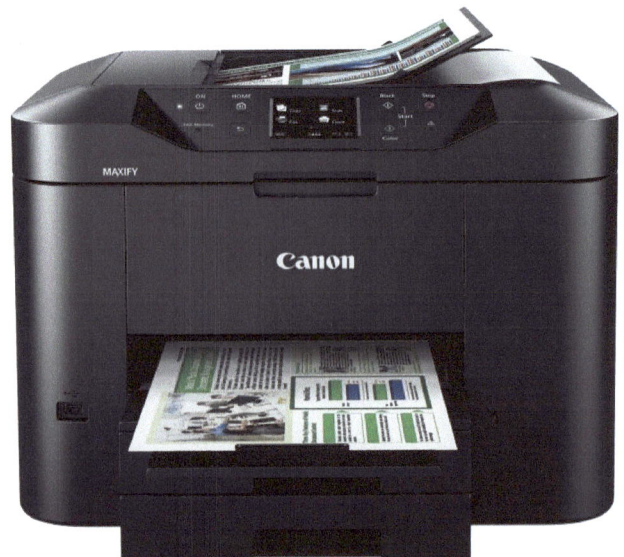

Yeezy Runoffs with the Copyrights

THE INDUSTRY DOESN'T SLY AWAY FROM TAKING PRISONERS WHEN IT COMES TO COPYRIGHT INFRINGEMENT EVEN IF YOUR KANYE WEST.

by Cheraee C.

The last thing any artist wants to be accused of is copyright theft. Unfortunately, for Kanye West, a copyright case for 2.5 million is pending against him by the victim who is an Hungarian rock singer named Gabor Presser. Gabor claims that Kanye sampled his work without his permission on his song 'New Slaves.' Exact claims are that the song 'New Slaves' is one-third of an unauthorized copy of the 1969 single Gyongyhaju Lany.

Apparently, Kanye's team tried to pay Gabor hush money with a 10,000 check and tried to reach out to Gabor by email. They tried to force his hand by giving him 24 hours to respond to their emails and desires to make a deal so the sampling wouldn't get messy. Before Gabor could even make a logical decision, Kanye had already started marketing and promoting the sample like music doesn't travel.

Presser is a composer and musician from the 60's era who had no idea that Kanye was boosting his song without his permission. Still Kanye, his lawyers, or Sony/ATV Music Publishing LLC are remaining silent on this one. Their probably trying to conjure up a masterplan or a settlement bigger then the first check they tried to give Presser.

Hopefully now, artists will be more careful on how they sample music and gain some patience because you can't rush perfection. Some projects take longer then others, and taking time is better then dealing with legal documents and court.

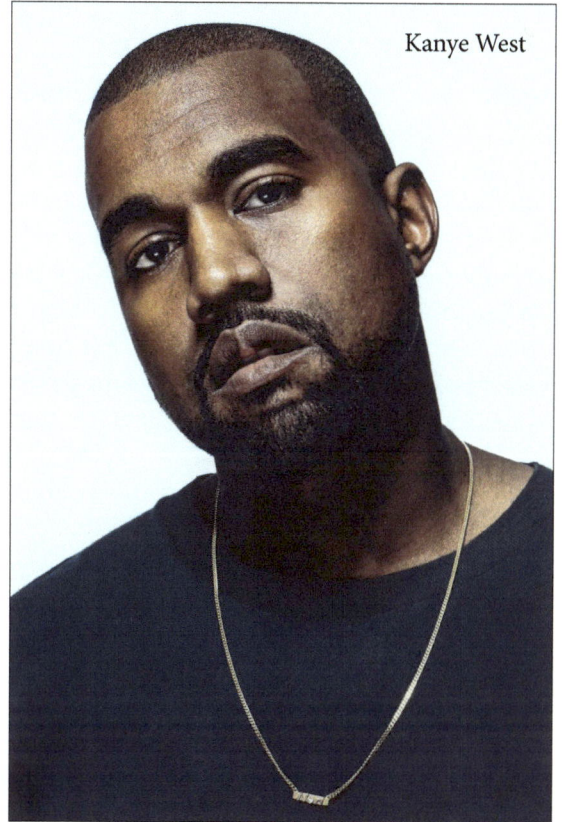

Kanye West

Who's Out For Vengeance?

URBAN BESTSELLING AUTHOR ZANE IS BACK WITH A MIND-RACING TALE OF VENGEANCE.

by Cheraee C.

Author Zane is best known for two of the greatest books in urban history which are Addicted and Nervous. From writing million dollar novels, to her Sex Chronicles series on Cinemax, to hitting theatre screens with the movie version of her book Addicted, Zane is back with another thriller titled Vengeance.

Zane, best known for her characters with personality issues/disorders takes us on a joyride with the popstar of her book Caprice Tatum who comes back to her hometown Atlanta as Wicket to seek revenge to everyone who caused her agony and grief in her past especially in the name of fame. Will she let the past go and get therapeutic help, or will she sink from the wrath of her own demise? Vengeance by Zane is a must read.

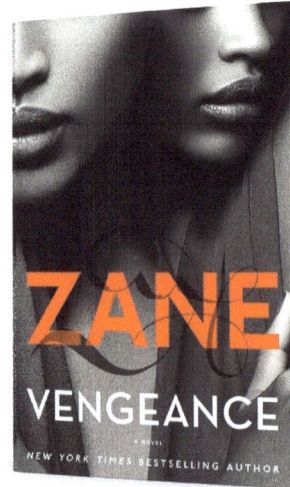

Vengeance
By Zane

Available from Amazon.com and other online stores

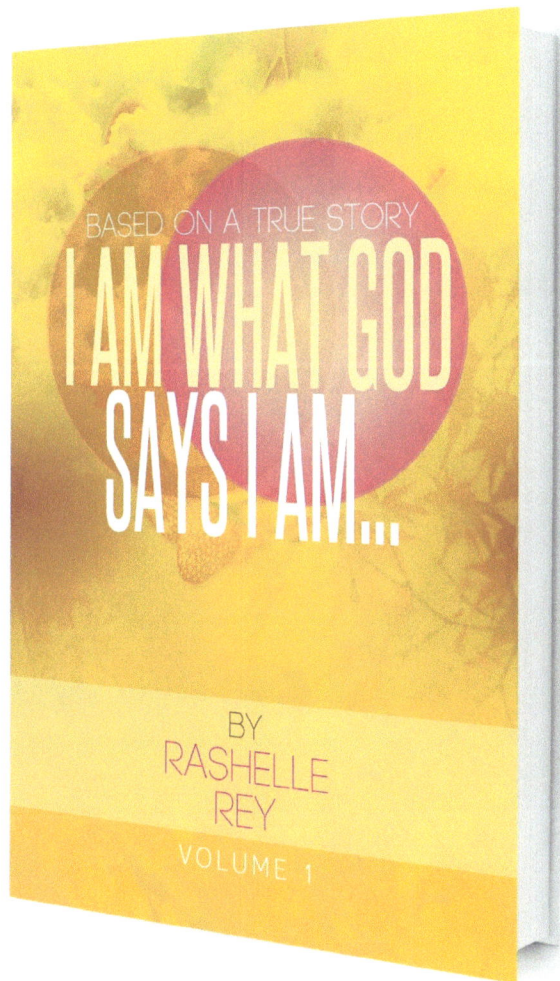

Making New Moves for Success

THE LEGENDARY ROCKSTAR CHRISTINA CHRISS BREAKS AWAY FROM HER GROUP KALEIDO TO EXPAND HER MUSIC CAREER AS A SOLO ARTIST.

by Cheraee C.

Q. Who is Christina Chriss as an artist and how did fame happen for you in the music industry?

A. I'm a free spirit. I love using my imagination and life experiences to create songs that I hope touch other's lives. I've been singing since I was 5 and music has been a part of my entire life. I started my band Kaleido and hit the ground running. I put 100% of my heart into my music and my performances, and that's what has gotten me to where I am right now. I'm just in love with what I'm doing and I think it speaks, it shows.

Q. What label are you signed too and how do you feel about labels in general? It is better being an unsigned artist or a signed artist?

A. I'm an independent artist. I think both independent and major labels are an incredible part of getting exposure.

Q. How did your band Kaleido come about and tell us a few things about the members in your band and how do they feel about you chasing your dreams as an solo artist?

A. I started Kaleido with my 4 very best friends Joey Fava, Ronnie Rosolino, Cody Morales, & Jamie Burnham. We all came up in music around Metro Detroit. We've grown together, we live together, write together, tour together - we're a family. We all make music together and separately and we support one another 100%. These guys are my team and they're all incredibly talented in so many ways. When our minds get together - it's fire.

Q. Out of all the great accomplishments you have made in your career so far, which accomplishment means the most to you?

A. Singing the National Anthem at the Detroit Tiger's game on my

veteran grandfather's 79th birthday... And he was there in person to see it! He passed away about a month ago, and I'm just so happy I was able to share that moment, that experience with him. He served in Germany with Elvis Presley, the stories are amazing, he was a total rockstar Grandpa.

Q. How was it working with Trick Trick and French Montana and who is Christina Chriss when your not doing music?

A. It was super fun. I love Trick Trick, he's been my friend for years, so we finally got to do a record together and he absolutely slays his verse. French was super chill, really nice guy, and we got a banger together - I can't wait to put it out. I gotta give a shout to Detail, my producer, for making it all come to life. He's super talented. Also my manager Mikey Eckstein & Adam Bleznak! Christina Chriss not doing music is reading about the universe and becoming the best person I can be every single day that I'm on this planet.

The Queen of Hip-Hop/R&B Radio

THE STREETS IS ALWAYS TALKING SO TUNE IN TO IKEISHA BAKER
ACROSS RADIO ONE STATIONS AND HER BRAND NEW MIXTAPE

by Cheraee C.

Q. Define who Ikeisha Baker is as an entrepreneur and what influenced you to do radio?

A. I am a down to earth person who has two sons I love dearly. I work in radio for Radio One Detroit Hot 107.5, Kiss 105.9, 120.0 WCHB Newstalk, and 102.7 Praise for over 6 years now. What influenced me to do radio, is my oldest son Darvin b.k.a Darko. I always had a passion for music coming up as a kid. When I was in high school...I took a Radio TV & Broadcasting class at Northwestern High School for 4 years. I was the News Anchor for "Colt Mania News" for the entire school. But, my son Darko started rapping at the age of 5 and writing his own music by the age of 7, and that was my main reason why I pursued my career in radio.

Q. How did you get your shot as a radio host and what is your opinion of the radio shows in Detroit?

I went to "Specs Howard", and during the time I was attending Specs...I was offered an internship position at Radio One Detroit. I grind so hard that they offered me a position with there company, and I have not turn back. I am base in the Promotion Department, I helped out Programming, and the Business Department. My opinion about the radio shows in Detroit...I think that they should keep all shows local, and stop doing syndicated shows from other places.

Q. Your mixtape movement "The Streets is Talking" just kicked off and your going to be running them back to back. What made you decide to create this mixtape?

A. I created the mixtape "The Streetz Is Talking" because, I want to showcase, and give exposure to the upcoming local hot artist that have talented but the city is sleeping on them due to them not being known or their brand is not build in the city. That's when I come in the play, by dropping mix tapes and doing my show every Friday at 2 am on Hot 107.5 "Hot In The Streets".

Q. How does a person go about getting on your mixtape and what makes your mixtape stand out to all the other million mixtapes floating around the D?

A. They can go to Sound Cloud, YouTube, or hit me up on Facebook, Twitter, or Instagram @ikeishabaker. What makes my mixtape stands out is because... I am showcasing up coming local hot artists. I am giving people a chance to exposed their talented. I don't just throw people on my mixtape. I have them email me their track, and I screen their song before it goes on my mixtape. If the song meet's up to my standards, I give them an opportunity to book a slot on my mixtape.

Q. What are your views on underground music and mainstream music? Do you prefer one over the other?

A. I prefer both. When you are in the entertainment world, and doing radio, you need to know about the underground scene, and mainstream stream music. Majority of rappers, and singers who are famous today started off doing underground, and than become mainstream artists. It's always good to follow the underground scene because it keeps you in the loop on who my be the next thing to blow.

Leading Detroit To Hollywood

SHAWN P IS ASPIRING ACTORS/ACTRESSES TO HIT THE STAGE
AND FOCUSING ON MAKING DETROIT OUR OWN HOLLYWOOD

by Cheraee C.

Q. How did Shawn P become a producer and what led to the start and the rise of Shawn P Entertainment?

A. My journey as a producer and playwright began over 10 years ago when I was in charge of the "Drama Ministry – Vision of Hope" at my church, Joseph Campau Avenue Church of God. I had a number of supporters who encouraged me to expand beyond the walls of the church. I began to seek out theaters so more people would have access to my plays! My first play was "Church Folks?!" in 2006 written by Lanette M. White (the concept was originated by me) and from there it took off.

Q. Shawn, you are known for the plays, so in your eyes, what is the most popular play that you produced so far and why?

A. The most popular play I ever produced was "The Vagina Monologue: V-Day" written by Eve Ensler, the Tony-winning playwright. Radio Host Frankie Darcell of WMXD - 92.3 FM, introduced me to the play and inspired me to produce it. The stage play is such a powerful play that elevates the conversation on the feminine experience, which touches on sex, love, rape, birth and the various names of the vagina. I am forever, grateful to Frankie. I think 'The Vagina Monologues' speaks to a lot of people not just women, but men too. This play touches so many people's lives. V-Day is a global non-profit movement that has raised over $100 million for groups working to end violence against women and girls anti-violence through benefits of Vagina Monologues.

Q. What is your current opinion about the entertainment sector in Detroit as it relates to acting, plays, playwrights, films, and producers?

A. This is an exciting time for Detroit entertainment as it relates to acting, plays, playwrights, films, and producers! Detroit has so many talented people doing great things in the city. As an entertainment community in Detroit we need to help and support each other more. Actors need to actively promote each other and encourage each other more, plus buy tickets. Detroiters as a whole have to support Detroit artists more: Detroit plays, Detroit films, Detroit music etc.

Q. You love working with the people in Detroit so why does Detroit mean so much to you and why only limit your candidates to Detroiters?

A. I am not limiting myself to only working with Detroiters. I am open to teaming up and working with anyone in entertainment. Right now the focus is on Detroit…we want to make Detroit our own Hollywood! We should not have to run to LA, Hollywood, Chicago, or Atlanta when we have our own Mecca of entertainment right here in Detroit. We Detroiters may not be operating on a grand level as Hollywood, however, Detroit's plays and films can compete with some of the nationally run companies.

Q. Your always cooking up a play so what play will you be coming out with next and when!

A. I am currently promoting "One Story, One Mic" featuring local Detroiters who have a story to tell in a provocative way! Everyone has a story to share and it's all about how they are going to tell it! "One Story, One Mic" stage production will be held October 2, 2016 at 4:00 p.m. at the International Institute – 111 E. Kirby, Detroit, Michigan 48202. For more information contact shawnpentertainment@gmail.com or call (313) 433-8384. Photography by April Smiley.

Welcome to the DollHouse

SIX EXTRAVAGANT DOLLS ARE READY TO CHANGE THE FACE OF THE
INDUSTRY WITH CLASS, MOTIVATION, AND A SKIN TIGHT SISTERHOOD

by Cheraee C.

Q. Who created Dollhouse Media Group, and why do you choose
to refer to your girls as dolls?

A. I (Precious Houston) created DollHouse with a friend of mine
after having a bad experience/separation from another female promotion group. I refer to them as "Dolls" because we are DollHouse
lol but, because it was a term of endearment that helped create the
group.

Q. Who are all the members in the Dollhouse and what specific
talent or attribute scored them as a doll?

A. There are 6 members including myself. Shelby is a
Medical Assistant/aspiring model. Ariel is also a Medical Assistant,
model, skater, and up and coming actress. Kearra is a photogra-
pher, model, promoter, marketing specialist, and mother. Kenyatta
is an up an coming HOT artist and model. Honey is a model,
former artist, promoter, and mother. Precious (myself) is a Medical Administrative Assistant, Fleet Coalition Model, Entrepreneur,
actress, student, and mother. We are all around movers and shak-
ers in the entertainment world.

Q. How do you recruit and choose members in the Dollhouse? Is it
a certain look or status that you have to embody to be recruited?

A. I get a ton of girls who ask about being in the DollHouse.
Honestly, I involve all my members in the recruitment process.
Everyone gives their opinion. I like someone who has great work
ethic, motivation, team member skills, a great look, and attitude.

Doesn't need to be a specific look. I like all different kinds of women,
they just need to be able to own their personality and embrace the
personalities of other DollHouse members.

Q. What type of commitment comes with being in the Dollhouse? Is
it a lifelong commitment or just a stepping stone to elevate a person's
career?

A. Being in the DollHouse is most definitely a stepping stone for someone's career, I love to see people move up and move on to bigger and
better opportunities, but the sisterhood and bond we all have with one
another is for a lifetime!

Q. Who is Dollhouse affiliated with, where are the members of
Dollhouse from, and what's the biggest goal for Dollhouse?

A. The DollHouse is the sister company to Victory ENT, which is
headed by Jay Lavon and Johnny "J" Hustle. Most of the members are
from Michigan with the exception of Ariel who is from Delaware.
The biggest goal right now for DollHouse is to get our names and im-
ages out to the public more and more. We also have a goal to promote
sisterhood and teamwork to other women following our lead. We want
to bring the entertainment world something new and exciting, everyone
can participate in and relate to! We want to pack out these venues and
see everyone having a great time with no drama! DollHouse Sunday's
starts on June 12 at Study Hall Lounge in Ann Arbor. It's a day party
EVERY SUNDAY! Make sure you're there! Tell your friends!

Spotify Doing Numbers

STREAMING COMPETITION IS HEATING UP AS SPOTIFY REVENUES SKY ROCKET

by Semaja Turner

Spotify is reportedly the world's largest and greatest streaming service company in comparison with Apple Music and Tidal, and all the upcoming streaming companies sitting under the radar. Spotify's revenues have reportedly exceeded more than 1.5 billion dollars even after it did major investing to abominate the competition. Of course, Tidal and Apple Music are always innovating something new to increase their status in the streaming world, but right now Spotify is the top dog.

There are so many advantages when it comes to Spotify; who wouldn't want to subscribe with them? Spotify is an international streaming service who has recently added Indonesia as it's 59th country to join the Spotify saga. Spotify also joined forces with Starbucks in the United States to reel in new subscribers.

In addition to that, Spotify created Discover Weekly which prompts a personalized playlist of songs, but now Discover Weekly offers video and podcast features.

Global digital music revenues are on the rise, and it's no stopping Spotify who plans to keep reinventing itself over and over again. No point in criticizing it's music streaming movement, mine as well just become a Spotify user.

Detroit's #1 Street King Returns

THE WAVE IS COMING BACK TO THE STREETS OF THE D AS KING DILLON RELEASES HIS HIGHLY ANTICIPATED ALBUM "THE CORONATION"

by Cheraee C.

Q. Dillion, better known in the industry as King Dillion, you are the true definition of an independent artist so what drives your quest for knowledge and independence in the music world?

A. Thank you, the desire to be a independent artist actually came from my mistakes! Starting off in the music industry I always had A "Team" behind me. I even started surrounding myself with people that I seen potential in over the years. I had people engineering music, promoting events, designing artwork, and everything else you can think of. Reality hit when some friendships went bad, people didn't have the time, or people just couldn't see eye to eye, and I had to literally start to learn how to become self sufficient. I waited for a long time and sat on so much music, until I realized, the dream don't stop for nobody. Another thing is, people are a little selfish when it comes to music knowledge, simply because they don't want you to be better than them. I swear to you everything I learned came from YouTube. I studied ProTools, Final Cut Pro, and I'm studying PhotoShop more right now actually. That's just how you eliminate the gaps between you and your goal. Now I can sit down and record a whole album, make a promo-pic to promote my single, and be able to get my video shot and edit it how I'd like it to be.

Q. Coming from a place where your music career was on top of the world, and then slowly dwindling down, how did King Dillon lose his focus in the music and how do you plan to keep it this time around?

A. Like I mentioned I just got caught up in the hype. It's all good... it happens to the best of us. I just wasn't focused on "myself." I was to busy worried about how "we" gon do this. I gotta get myself right before I can help anybody else. One thing about it though, that's why I grind for the people who still rock with me until this day. I get people on Twitter, Facebook, Instagram, and YouTube hitting me up in my DM and comments telling me to bring the wave back. But it's here now. We not letting up no more, we going all in this time around, plus I got a lot on the table lined up for this year and 2017! Be ready, because nothing is stopping this.

Q. When you first hit the music scene in 2008 you hit the radio hard with "The Problem" and in 2015 you did it again with the single "Friday," but suddenly you vanished. What happened to you?

A. That came from me not making any album since "19." I still made a lot of music, some on my SoundCloud even, but I never had a single to push. I've had mixtapes in between the period though. None with any song I pushed, or even got edited anyway.

Q. What is your opinion of the industry now that you have experienced disappointments and saw how labels, management, promoters, and friends act when you're at your high then drop to your low?

A. Well, I really don't feel any type of way about it to be honest with you. The way the universe worked out, I feel like I still have the upper-hand which lets me know I can go even higher than before, especially knowing what I know now. It was cool to be around it though, and it's not even like I'm saying that situation held me up completely. I just learned to go get it, elevate your craft, go beyond borders, and keep all your moves quiet. I was meant to be this artist I am today, so it's like a "Thanks! I needed that."

Q. Why do you choose to take full control of your music as far as the production goes, beats, and just the whole nine yards these days?

A. Because I don't have a certain style. It's hard to find someone to get your music to sound the way you hear it in your head. My music style is very random and unorthodox. I make music based on how I feel at any moment. I actually get a thrill off of being able to control my sound waves now and put them out for the world to hear. When people sit back and listen to it and actually rock with you, you know those 5 hours you spent staying up perfecting the mix, and laying those vocals were well worth it.

Q. Coronation means to crown him or her, so what's special about the release date and what is the inspiration for your new album titled 'The Coronation'?

A. "The Coronation" (6.1.16) is the second album I have released now, my first album was "Dillon-19." After, that my mixtape "Royalty 93" dropped, I changed my name to "King Dillon" to reinvent myself. My flow got crazy, my bars started tightening up, and my style was pure. This (The Coronation) will be my first album I've dropped since changing my name, so this is like the crowning of a new King. A new sound, a new look, a whole new approach.

Q. With a fresh new start, what's your plans this time around?

A. To give everybody what they want to hear, keep good music, and real bars coming. I'm not hearing no more real bars on the radio or nowhere, so I know it's time for me to turn up as far as this industry goes. I got it in a bag.

KING DILLON
the coronation

TOP 10 CHARTS

TOP 10 DIGITAL SINGLES AND ALBUMS
JUNE 1, 2016

TOP 10 CHARTS

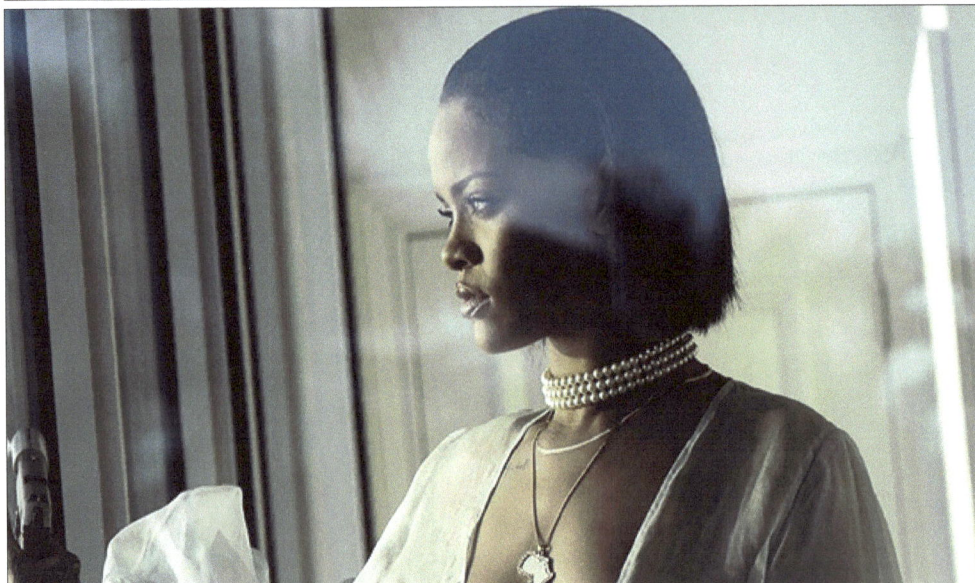

DESIIGNER IS ONE OF THE YOUNGEST RAPSTARS OUT TODAY WITH HIS NEW SINGLE "PANDA".

TOP 10 SINGLES
CHART OF THE MONTH

No.	Artist - Song Title
1	RIHANNA - NEEDED ME
2	DRAKE - KEEP THE FAMILY CLOSE
3	BEYONCE - LEMONADE
4	KING DILLON - WILT
5	ESKO - WHITE LINE FEVA
6	DESIIGNER - PANDA
7	KOSTA - TONIGHT FT. RICH MOOK
8	DRAKE - KEEP THE FAMILY CLOSE
9	MOBDIVA - RICH AND FAMOUS
10	CHRIS BROWN - GRASS AIN'T GREENER

TOP 10 ALBUMS
CHART OF THE MONTH

No.	Artist - Album Title
1	DRAKE - VIEWS
2	RIHANNA - ANTI
3	DAVID BANNER - BEFORE THE BOX
4	BRYSON TILLER - TRAPSOUL
5	BIG SEAN/JHENE AIKO - TWENTY88
6	KANYE WEST - THE LIFE OF PABLO
7	KEVIN GATES - ISLAH
8	TWEET - CHARLENE
9	KOSTA - D.I.Y
10	KING DILLON - THE CORONATION

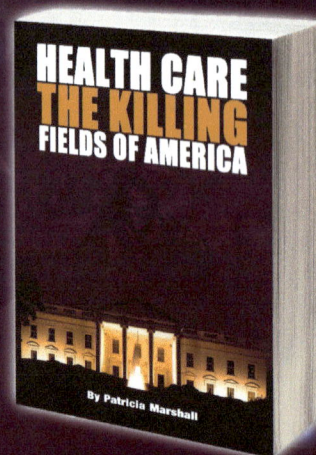

ALBUM REVIEW

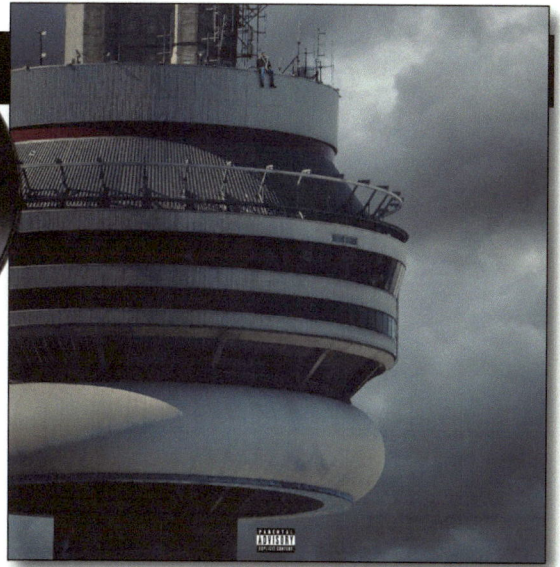

Views

ARTIST: Drake
REVIEWER: Cheraee C.
RATING: 5

All spring Drake has been preparing us for the dopest songs that will be banging through the Summer 2016. It started off with a dose of Hotline Bling, then he us with Redemption. If you ever heard a Drake album, then you know you can let the whole album play without skipping a song. Other tracks include Keep the Family Close, Too Good featuring Rihanna, Fire and Desire, Controlla, Child's Play, Grammy's featuring Future, and many more tracks. I give this album five stars.

RATE METER: 1 - WACK   2 - NEEDS WORK   3 - STRAIGHT   4 - BANGER   5 - CLASSIC

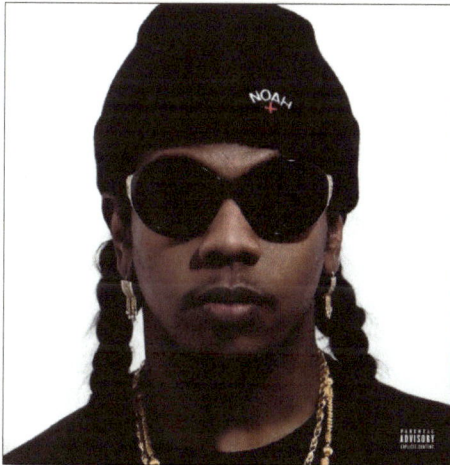

Trappy Mother's Day

ARTIST: Trinidad James
REVIEWER: Cheraee C.
RATING: 2

Just three years ago, Trinidad James had everybody talking about All Gold Everything. Now he's grinding hard on his music, but he's playing it by views. Who releases a mixtape with only three songs, and adds songs to a mixtape by using Youtube views as a scale? Tracks on this short mixtape include Still Aware, Still Hustlin, and Still Trill. I give this mixtape 2 stars.

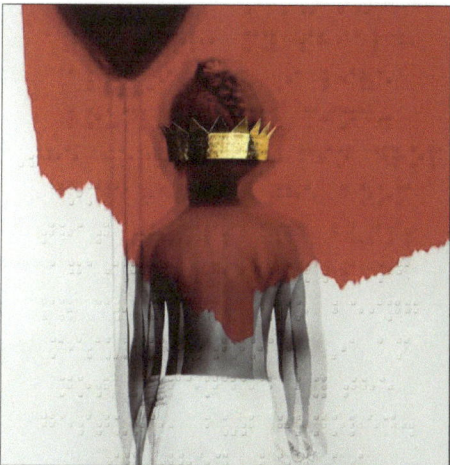

Anti

ARTIST: Rihanna
REVIEWER: Cheraee C.
RATING: 4

On a Ri-Ri album, you can always expect her to put your emotions in overdrive just like she does on her album Anti. Tracks from this album include Woo, Yeah, I Said It, Needed Me, Work, Desperado, and many other tracks. I give this album four stars.

HEELS &
SKILLZ

Shiyequa
is a full-time model
from Detroit, MI.
My hobbies are reading,
designing clothes and
shoes, and being with
my family.

instagram
@iam_bab_e

Photography by
@Jayjones

HEELS &
SKILLZ

Jessica Suzanne

is a beautiful model from Detroit, MI.
instagram
@jessicasuzanne3

HEELS & SKILLZ

Da Truth is a sexy model for barearmy and lives in Detroit, MI.

instagram
@DATRUTH101

Photography by
@barearmy

Cheraee's Corner
WHY DO PEOPLE LIE WHEN THEIR IN A RELATIONSHIP?
by Cheraee C.

Regardless of gender, lying when your in a relationship is really elementary. So many of us are aging while our mentalities and emotions remain youthful and in another realm. Relationships come with standards and obligations and if you not ready to oblige to those means why even enter a relationship?

The key to a healthy relationship is communication and unless you want your
relationship in the dysfunctional zone then, you should be truthful and afraid to lie to your partner. Yet people lie so much in a relationship, lying becomes an everyday habit like smoking. Nines out of ten, if you got to lie, your either in places or with people that you shouldn't be with, violating yourself and your relationship. The number one line, "I knew you would get mad if I told you the truth." Knowing that confirms that you know your partner, so you should know lying only hinders a person's feelings. People need to understand when you enter a relationship, your lifestyle changes completely. You can't do single things, you can't run the streets, and you have to respect your partner and their wishes.

Real women/men don't lie because they don't need to. Real people speak up about their feelings and take a stand in their relationship especially when they don't want to lose, upset, or disappoint their partner. Let's stop these men/women from having trust issues and just be truthful because a small lie only leads to a bigger lie, and nobody should want the reputation of being a liar on their conscious or associated with their name and legacy. Telling the truth is easy; it's the people that complicate the truth that make it hard trying to twist it, fabricate it, and bend it. You either truthful or your not and if your not truthful, stay far away from relationships and commitments. In some cases, lying can lead to death, so let's not live in the moment and try to defer away from consequences. You either giving or going to give your relationship 100% and above that or your not.

NEXT 2 BLOW

VEEZU

Q. All rappers have stories about the artist names they choose so what's the story about your name?

A. My name is just a spin on my real name. My birth name is Javon, so when I was in school everybody had rap names because everybody rapped lol. I remember being in the moment trying to find the right name to use. I came up with Young Jay, Javee, Javeezy, Javeezu, and so on... I didn't really like any of the names, but Javeezu stuck with me. All my close acquaintances at the time started calling me Javeezu and I ran with it. One day I got bold and just dropped the Ja and ran with Veezu by itself.

Q. Is rapping your only or main ambition or do you have other ambitions of value?

A. Rapping and just making great music overall is one of my multiple ambitions, but it's what I'm most passionate about.

Q. Just yesterday, rapping was just a dream so how does it feel to be progressing in the industry?

A. Honestly, I feel like it's still a dream. There's still more levels to hit, there's still more to come. I'm nowhere near the level I see myself, so I'd say the feeling is the same as it was just yesterday.

Q. If you could change anything about hip hop in today's society what would you change?

A. I would change the identity crisis in hip hop because of the lack of love for self and love for the art. People will do whatever for fame and money; it's starting to seem like it's more about that now a days.

Q. Who is Shiyequa the model? When did you first start modeling and what led you down the modeling path?

A. Shiyequa is my foundation; she who made me. I started modeling at about 13 years old. My mom took me to a model agency and they said I was too short for runway lol but, had the face for commercial. I really decided I wanted to take my modeling serious June 2015.

Q. Besides modeling, you also act so name a few videos and films that you've been in and tell us what it's like playing these roles and being filmed?

A. Oh gosh I'm currently working on CITY BOSS with Ball Out Boys Filmz BOB FILMZ starring Icewear Vezzo the creators of the movie SNAKE coming this summer in theatres everywhere July 4th. Also, I'm working on Deceitful Family ZHUGANG are the creators of that also coming in theatres this summer everywhere. You can catch me in those films and also The Good Guy, a horror film by William Bessant aka Dolla Bill. I'm currently getting ready to feature in videos just waiting on my manager call lol. I love acting just being someone I'm not is always dope. I have a good time on set; all the cast are extremely laid back and cool. When those cameras running, I'm so not myself I could do this for the rest of my life. I did the quick n weave commercial for go Detroit magazine and I'm also getting ready to do Royal Dynasty's lingerie spread in their magazine.

Q. Between modeling and acting which one do you prefer to do the most or they both equally important to you?

A. Modeling and acting are both a main priority in my life I started off modeling if I wasn't modeling I wouldn't be acting it's all about starting off somewhere modeling built a standard for me I took that and turned it into more so of a lifestyle and here I am working, booking like crazy I love it.

Q. Would you say there are peak seasons in modeling and acting or are they just all year around hustles?

A. Honestly. if I can not be real with myself, I can't be real with nobody. This game it's all about what you make of it. Yes it's hard, yes I cry, yes I wanna give up but, it's about chasing your goals and having understanding to your success and I'm humble and patient. I just wanna win lol.

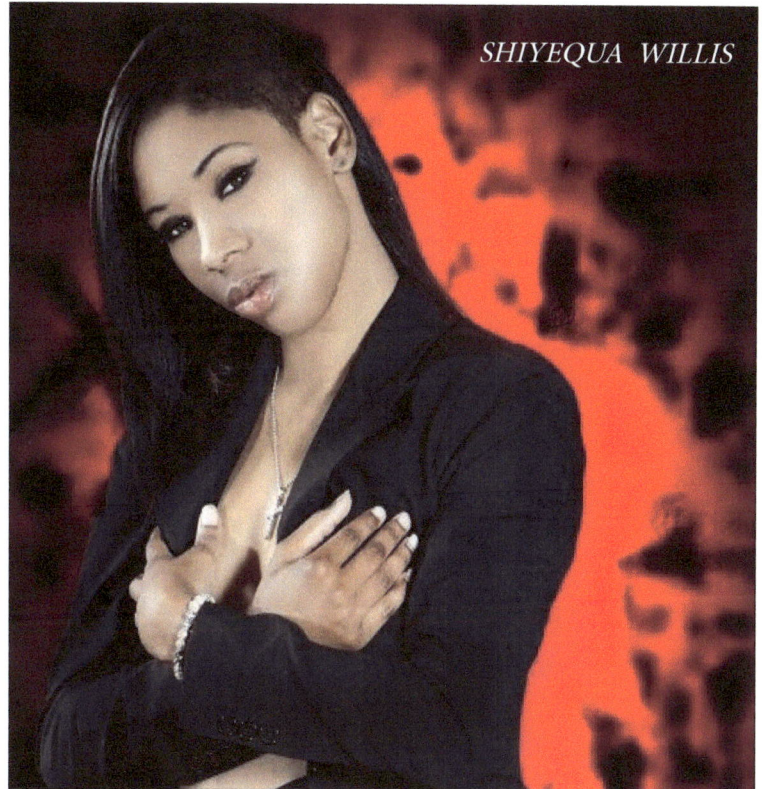

SHIYEQUA WILLIS

Q. How did you find out about SDM Magazine and how does it feel to be expanding to other states and cities?

A. I found out about SDM magazine from of course social media mainly my Instagram. I was wondering like damn how I get in this magazine? My dude was like reach out baby and ask them. Knowing me I take chances off the strength of I live off the quote chances make champions and here I am having this awesome interview with you guys. Expansion is always a plus it's beautiful. I need to keep my face out here as much as possible so I always been out my lead. Sometimes I feel I'm too much for myself lol, I love finding myself and conquering my obstacles

Q. As an entrepreneur, how do you balance motherhood with modeling and acting and what other talents do you have?

A. Story of my life but i can make it short for you when they say LIGHTS, CAMERA, ACTION, im working but im in mommy mode cause i do this for my babies they are my light they bring the cameras and im all action because im a mother before anything don't get me wrong i want them to have all my time i sometimes want them on set but in the long run they will understand mommy did this for you i dont live for me it's not about me i bust my buns for my babies and yes i do have other talents unfortunately i design custom shoes for children im currently working on my website but you can check out some pieces on my social media pages dope iish lol love it another passion i have i actually started before modeling and acting its been about 6 years for my custom line so yes check me out.

SNAP SHOTS

SNAP SHOTS

SNAP SHOTS

Email Your Snap Shots to
snapshots@sdmlive.com

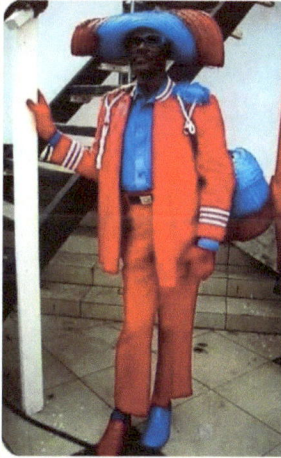

5DS PRODUCTIONS®
THE PRINT MEDIA CENTER.

PRINT

GET 10% OFF WITH CODE: SAVE10OFF

DIGITAL & PRESS RUN PRICE LIST

BUSINESS CARD
2x3.5 INCHES

100	$10
500	$20
1000	$30
5000	$100
10000	$170

TRIFOLD BROCHURE
8.5x11 INCHES

250	$150
500	$180
1000	$230
5000	$350
10000	$680

POSTCARDS
4x6 INCHES

250	$50
500	$55
1000	$65
5000	$130
10000	$250

**FLYERS - BROCHURES - BANNERS - BUSINESS CARDS - CD INSERTS
CALENDARS - EVENT TICKETS - POSTCARDS - POSTERS
YARD SIGNS - AND MUCH MORE**

DIGITAL & PRESS RUN PRINTING

FAST TURN AROUND PRINTING

GET FREE SHIPPING ON ALL ORDERS

YOU SAVE MONEY WHEN YOU PRINT AT
WWW.THEPRINTMEDIACENTER.COM
24/7 ONLINE ORDERING. CALL US NOW 1.888.718.2999

COUPON CODE IS FOR A LIMITED TIME OFFER - FREE UPS SHIPPING ANYWHERE IN THE US

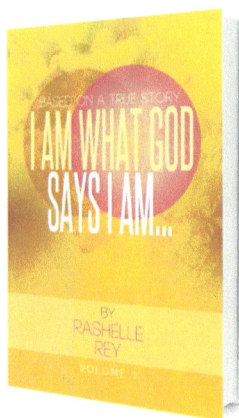

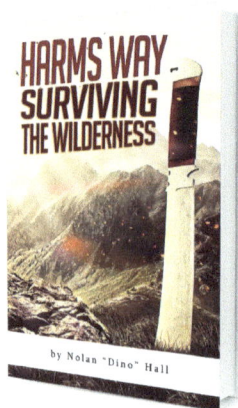

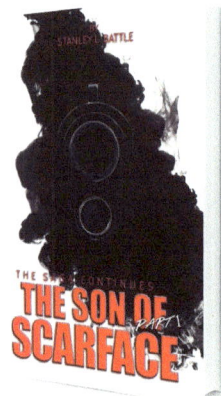

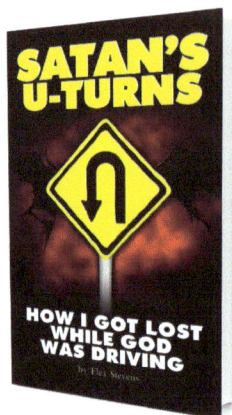

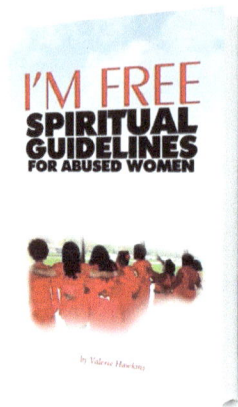

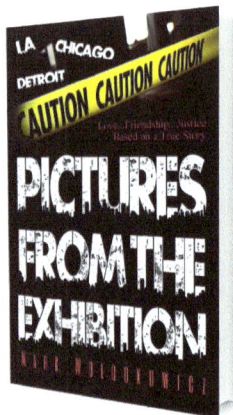

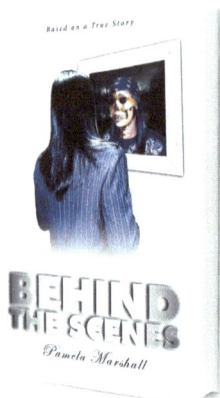

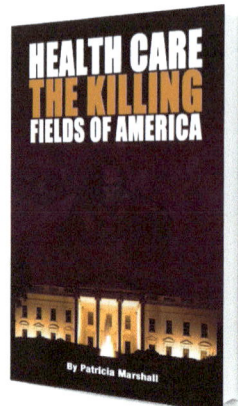

LOOKING FOR A NEW LOOK

LET US CREATE A NEW WEBSITE FOR YOUR COMPANY FOR LESS.

Basic

$3.99/month

1 Website
10 GB Storage
25,000 Monthly Vistors

PLUS

* FREE Monthly Hosting

* Get a FREE Domain
with annual plan

Standard

$4.99/month

1 Website
15 GB Storage
100,000 Monthly Vistors

PLUS

* FREE Monthly Hosting

* Search engine
optimization plugin

* Get a FREE Domain
with annual plan

Premium

$12.99/month

1 Website
50 GB Storage
800,000 Monthly Vistors

PLUS

* FREE Monthly Hosting

* Search engine
optimization plugin

* RapidSSL Certificate

* Get a FREE Domain
with annual plan

We offer complete WordPress website design and development. From a simple website to an advanced business e-Commerce solution, we can create the ultimate solution to meet your marketing goals and objectives.

All of our custom website builds follow a structured development process which helps us execute your project on-time and on-budget. For prices go to www.5DShost.com/websites

5DSHOST
THE BEST FOR HOSTING

Call Our Support:
(888) 718-2999
WWW.5DSHOST.COM